ALL THE PAINTINGS OF
BOTTICELLI

Part 2

VOLUME TWENTY-SIX
in the
Complete Library of World Art

The Complete Library of World Art

ALL THE PAINTINGS

OF **BOTTICELLI**

Part 2 (1445–1484)

By ROBERTO SALVINI

Translated from the Italian by
JOHN GRILLENZONI

HAWTHORN BOOKS, INC.
Publishers · *New York*

Printed and bound in Great Britain by
Jarrold & Sons Ltd, Norwich

CONTENTS

BOTTICELLI'S PAINTINGS

Plate 62

MADONNA OF THE SEA. *Panel, 40.3 × 28.4. Florence, Accademia.* Originally in the Convent of Santa Felicita in Florence. Ulmann thought it might be a Botticelli, but the over-painting made a final judgment impossible. Van Marle ascribed it to "Sandro's friend." Gamba considered it a Botticelli, close in time to the *Raczinsky Tondo,* despite its poor condition. Procacci catalogued it as a school product. Some critics have tried unconvincingly to attribute it to Filippino Lippi. As Gamba has pointed out, this is a delicate devotional image by Botticelli, in which the Verrocchio and Pollaiuolo elements are dissolved in a way which anticipates the *Primavera.*

Plate 63

RACZINSKY TONDO. *Panel, diameter 135. Berlin, Staatliche Museen.* Originally in the Raczinsky Collection in Berlin. Vasari records "a *tondo* with a Madonna and with life-size angels, which was considered quite beautiful" in the present Church of San Salvatore al Monte. Later he added that there were eight angels in another similar *tondo* executed by a follower. Since this is the only *tondo* we can ascribe to Botticelli with eight angels, it was thought that the *tondo* must have been the one in San Francesco (San Salvatore). But the evidence is tenuous. Many scholars think it a workshop product. Others think it is only partly autograph. Dates are hazarded in a wide range, from 1475 to the 1490s.

I think the high quality is un-deniable and Botticellian. Rather than attributing the archaic aspects to the workshop, I would prefer, considering the lighter use of Pollaiuolo elements, to date it around the time of the *Adoration of the Magi* in the Uffizi (plate 52), around 1477.

Plates 64–65

PRIMAVERA. *Panel, 203 × 314. Florence, Uffizi Gallery.* The *Anonimo Gaddiano* refers to the painting in describing Giovanni de' Medici's collection: ". . . at Castello, [Botticelli] painted more canvases, which are among the best he has ever done, in Giovanni de' Medici's house . . ." Vasari (1550 and 1568) cites "two pictures representing the birth of Venus . . . and another Venus being crowned with flowers by the Graces, denoting spring . . ." in the "villa of Duke Cosimo." The painting is de-scribed as being in the villa at Castello by the inventories of 1598 and 1638. It was taken to the Uffizi in 1815, transferred to the Accademia in 1864, and definitively returned to the Uffizi in 1919. At first, scholars thought it had been painted for Lorenzo the Magnificent, but later research revealed that the villa at Castello had been purchased in 1477 for Lorenzo and Giovanni di Pier-francesco de' Medici and passed on to their heirs, Giovanni delle Bande Nere, and then Duke Cosimo I, his son. The *Anonimo* refers to Giovanni, and Vasari to his son. The painting was probably executed, therefore, as a decoration for the villa and begun in 1477. Critics generally agree with Cavalcaselle's dating of 1478. If the quality of the *Primavera* is higher, the difference, in terms of idiom, from *The Adoration of the Magi* is imperceptible and justifies a dating of 1477-78. On the other hand, we can still clearly see that the basis of *Primavera* is the functional linearity of Pollaiuolo (Horne points out the similarity to Pollaiuolo's *Birth of St John the Baptist* on the silver altar in the Works of the Duomo), while we cannot find a trace of Andrea del Castagno's monumentality that will mark the *St Augustine* (1480) in Ognissanti. Since the occasion for imitating Andrea del Castagno—as most critics agree—was offered to Botticelli when he was asked to paint some frescoes illustrating the punishment of the Pazzi conspirators (a subject very similar to that which Castagno had painted on the tower of the Palazzo del Podestá), we can assume that the *Primavera* was painted at the latest in the early part of 1478. The frescoes with the Pazzi conspirators was painted, we know, between April 26, 1478 and July 21, 1478 (the date in which he received payment). Since the *Primavera* shows no sign of Andrea del Castagno's forceful style, we are compelled to our conclusion by circumstantial evidence.

Interpretation of the theme has long occupied scholars' attention. Warburg (1893) proposed that the subject derived from Poliziano, or was suggested directly; that is, from Ovid and other classic stories—the theme could be "The Reign of Venus." Zephyr on the right pursues Flora, possesses her and then marries her, granting her the power to turn whatever she touches into flowers. Then follows the Hour of Spring (Flora transformed by Zephyr), Venus at the center, then the three Graces and Mercury. The interpretation is essentially right, and certainly preferable to Jacobsen's, in which the allegory functions to commemorate the dead Simonetta, with Zephyr as Death, and the scene as Elysium, where she is reborn. The earlier interpretation is preferable even to Gombrich's ingenious attempt to read this scene as the aftermath of Paris' judgment, as described in Apuleius' *The Golden Ass* (Venus, he adds, is the symbol of Humanity, according to a letter written by Ficino to the very young Pierfrancesco de' Medici). There are even simple interpretations, for instance, Battisti's (1954) according to which the painting represents the cycle of the seasons, with the months embodied by the various figures; e.g. Zephyr is February, Mercury September. A very recent interpretation, rather elaborate and difficult to accept, would find a political allegory here, along with the *Stanze* of Poliziano. Welliver claims that the painting is an exhortation to Giuliano de' Medici to seek a cardinalate from Pope Sixtus IV. We tend to accept Gombrich's identification of Venus as Humanity (without going as far as specifying *The Golden Ass*), and thus the painting is an allegory of the kingdom of Venus, of an ideal world where nature and instinct, embodied by the erotic Zephyr and Flora, are ennobled by culture and civilization, embodied by Venus (Humanity) accompanied by the Graces. The latter are interpreted in several ways in humanistic texts, but always considered the daughters of Venus, or as the three aspects of the goddess. Ficino's Venus is also accompanied by Mercury, whom he identifies as good advice, reason or knowledge. The interpretation has the advantage of being analogous to the allegory of *Pallas and the Centaur* (plate 113).

Plate 66

PRIMAVERA. Detail: the three Graces.

Plate 67

PRIMAVERA. Detail of plate 66.

Plate 68

PRIMAVERA. Detail of plate 67.

Color Plate I

PRIMAVERA. Detail of plates 64–65.

Plate 69

PRIMAVERA. Detail of plate 67.

Plate 70

PRIMAVERA. Detail of plate 66, the upper part.

Plate 71

PRIMAVERA. Detail: Mercury's head.

Plate 72

PRIMAVERA. Detail: Flora and Zephyr.

Plate 73

PRIMAVERA. Detail: Primavera's head.

Plate 74

PRIMAVERA. Detail: the figure of Primavera.

Plate 75

PRIMAVERA. Detail: the figure of Primavera.

Plate 76

PRIMAVERA. Detail: Love aims his arrow.

Plate 77

PRIMAVERA. Detail: the greenery in the upper left.

Plate 78

ST AUGUSTINE. *Fresco, 152 × 112. Florence, Church of Ognissanti.* The earliest mention is in the *Memoriale* by Albertini (1510), who notes a "St Dominic [*sic*]" by Ghirlandaio and a "St Jerome [*sic*]" by Botticelli in the Ognissanti. The *Libro di Antonio Billi* (Petrei Codex) cites "a St Augustine in Ognissanti, on a pillar of the front choir . . ." and the *Anonimo Gaddiano* confirms this, adding that the fresco faced a *St Jerome,* both of which had been painted in a competition at the same time. Vasari tells us that Botticelli was commissioned by the Vespucci, and that he was competing with Ghirlandaio. When the choir was demolished in 1564, the two frescoes were detached and rearranged on the walls of the nave, where they may still be seen. The Ghirlandaio is dated 1480, and if we are to believe all the sources, the Botticelli fresco should be dated the same year. The Vespucci seal confirms Vasari's account; Horne thinks the donor was Anastasio Vespucci, Amerigo's father. Critics have noted Andrea del Castagno's influence, which Van Marle denies (1931).

Plate 79

ST AUGUSTINE. Detail: bust of the Saint.

Plate 80

SAN MARTINO ANNUNCIATION. *Detached fresco, 243 × 550. Florence, Exhibition of Frescoes in the Belvedere.* The fresco comes from the Church of San Martino della Scala, where it was located on the upper part of the right wall over the entrance. The entrance, or atrium, used to be the loggia of the San Martino Hospital. The hospital was, according to Horne, built in 1313 as a dependency of the Hospital of Santa Maria della Scala in Siena, it was suppressed in 1536 and is now a reform school. In 1529, when the convent outside the walls was demolished before a siege, the nuns of San Martino delle Panche took shelter in the hospital, which was then ceded to them in 1531. In 1624, the loggia of the old hospital was remodeled as the entrance to the church. The upper part was made into a small choir for the nuns by building a single vault with two arches which divided the fresco into two lunettes. It was detached in 1920 and restored in 1952. Horne recognized it as Botticelli's work in 1908 and dated it around 1490. But Poggi found some documents which prove Botticelli did it during April and May 1481, before going to Rome. In the vigorous perspective we can see Andrea del Castagno's influence, while the rhythm of the line becomes more impetuous. Again we have some confirmation that the *Primavera* must have preceded this painting and the *St Augustine* (Uffizi) by a few years, if only in the difference to be seen in the quality of the line.

Plate 81a

SAN MARTINO ANNUNCIATION. Detail: the angel.

Plate 81b

SAN MARTINO ANNUNCIATION. Detail: the Virgin.

Plate 82

ST THOMAS AQUINAS. *Canvas, 47 × 35. Zurich, Alegg Stockar Collection.* Formerly in the Holford Collection, Gloucestershire. The painting has been various ascribed to Cosmé Tura, Montagna, Gentile Bellini, Bonsignori and Signorelli. A. Venturi recognized it as a Botti-

celli in 1922. He noted the close relationship to the *St Augustine* in the Church of Ognissanti (plate 78) on the one hand, and with the artist's Roman frescoes on the other (plates 84a–86c). The Holford Collection accepted the attribution in its catalog, and so did Yashiro, but he withdrew his acceptance later. Bettini, Gamba and Berenson agree with Venturi, even as to the date; that is, around 1481–82. Mesnil thinks Botticelli painted it around 1495, about the time he painted *Calumny* (Part 4, plates 92–93). Its high quality and the relationship with the *St Augustine* and with the portraits of the popes in the Sistine Chapel certainly make for a date around 1481.

Plate 83

MADONNA AND CHILD WITH ST JOHN THE BAPTIST. *Round panel, diameter 95. Piacenza, Museo Civico.* This *tondo* was taken from the Castello Bardi in 1860. Pollinari first described it as a Botticelli in 1890, and Ferrari published it as such in 1903. Some critics (Bode, Van Marle) think it a school product, and others tacitly reject it. Gamba considers it autograph, and dates it around the time of the *San Martino Annunciation* (1481). Berenson considered it a joint effort by Botticelli and his workshop. It is an extremely delicate work, certainly conceived and largely painted by Sandro. Probably datable around 1481.

Color Plate II

PRIMAVERA. Detail of plates 64–65.

FRESCOES IN THE SISTINE CHAPEL

Plates 84–105

The earliest mention of Botticelli's participation in the decoration of the Sistine Chapel is in the *Libro di Antonio Billi* (1516–30), but the relevant part of the book has been clumsily edited in the Petrei Codex. We read that "he did more pictures of small things in the Sistine Chapel, among others a St Jerome." Obviously the editor misread his source which may have indicated other paintings the artist did in Rome besides the frescoes in the chapel. The *Anonimo Gaddiano*, in fact, says that "he did three faces or pictures in Sixtus's chapel," and continues, "and many small, beautiful things, among them a singular St Jerome." Vasari describes the Sistine frescoes very generally: ". . . when Christ was tempted by the Devil; when Moses killed the Egyptian and was offered something to drink by Jethro's daughters; and when Aaron's sons were being sacrificed, fire came down from heaven . . . and several saintly popes in the niches above the stories." He claimed Botticelli was in charge of the chapel decorations. Gnoli and, later, Steinmann published documents which indicate that on October 27, 1481, Cosimo Rosselli, Ghirlandaio, Perugino and Botticelli contracted to paint scenes from the Old and New Testaments by March 15, 1482, for a sum to be based on the value of the scenes they had already painted. We gather from this that four frescoes had been painted, including the portraits of the popes. Afterwards, Signorelli, Pinturicchio and Piero di Cosimo were called in because the authorities decided to increase the number of scenes. Botticelli, it has been established, painted several of the popes and the three scenes Vasari describes, from around June 1481 (since he was painting the *San Martino Annunciation* in Florence in May) until March 1482. In fact, the custodians of the Signoria in Florence commissioned Ghirlandaio, Botticelli, Perugino, Biggio Tucci and Piero

del Pollaiuolo to decorate the Hall of Lilies on October 5, and the artists were indicated as being present. (Cf. Gaye, *Carteggio inedito*, I, 1840, and Mesnil in *Rivista d'Arte*, 1905.)

The central theme of the frescoes lay in the parallels to be found between the Old and New Testaments. Perugino, says Vasari, painted the *Finding of Moses* on the left, and the *Nativity* on the right. These frescoes were destroyed to make room for Michelangelo's. From the altar, there followed on the two walls *Moses Goes into Egypt* and the *Circumcision of the First Born* (on the left) and the *Baptism of Christ* (on the right) by Pinturicchio. Botticelli painted the *Trials of Moses* (left), and (right) *Temptation of Jesus* (plates 87 and 92). Ghirlandaio did the *Crossing the Red Sea* and the *Calling of Peter and Andrew* (right); Cosimo Rosselli painted *Moses on Mount Sinai* and *Sermon on the Mount and Healing of the Leper* (right). Botticelli painted the *Punishment of Korah* (left) and Perugino, *Delivery of the Keys* (right). The *Last Days of Moses* (left) is attributed to Signorelli, and Rosselli painted *The Last Supper and Passion of Christ* (right). On the wall over the entrance, there was the *Dispute of St Michael and Satan over Moses' Body* repainted by Matteo da Lecce in the sixteenth century, and the *Resurrection*, originally by Ghirlandaio (Vasari) but redone by Arrigo Fiammingo in the sixteenth century.

Botticelli obviously had to use helpers because of the limited time at his disposal; we can see this primarily in the portraits of the popes, (plates 84a–86c), while it is less evident in the three stories. That Fra Diamante and Filippino Lippi were among his helpers is improbable: Fra Diamante is mentioned in connexion with other frescoes and

Lippi, according to a contemporary report, had nothing to do with the frescoes in the chapel.

The portraits of the twenty-eight popes above the Biblical stories, as I have said, were done quickly, mostly by helpers. And they have been retouched and repainted much more frequently than the other frescoes. Criticism has thus been made difficult, and is seldom consistent. We are certain some of the portraits were done from Botticelli's drawings, some were done by the artist himself, and many can be attributed to Ghirlandaio and his pupils. The portraits published here are the ones in which we can clearly detect Botticelli's hand, even if some were partly done by other painters.

Plate 84a

POPE ST EVARISTUS. *Fresco, 260 × 85.*

Plate 84b

POPE ST CORNELIUS. *Fresco, 260 × 85.*

Plate 85a

POPE ST SIXTUS. *Fresco, 260 × 85.*

Plate 85b

POPE ST MARCELLINUS. *Fresco, 260 × 85.*

Plate 86a

POPE ST STEPHEN. *Fresco, 260 × 85.*

Plate 86b

POPE ST SOTER. *Fresco, 260 × 85.*

Plate 86c

POPE ST LUCIUS. *Fresco, 260 × 85.* Sometimes mistakenly referred to as "Voío."

Plate 87

SCENES FROM THE LIFE OF MOSES. *Fresco, 348 × 558, second section of the wall on the left.* Generally described as the stories of Moses' youth, the fresco concerns the preparation for his mission as a parallel to the next fresco showing the preparation of Christ. There are seven episodes: at the right, in the foreground, Moses kills the Egyptian who was beating the Jew, while toward the extreme right of the fresco a woman drags the wounded man away (Exodus, 2:11f.); behind, Moses' flight (Exodus, 2:15). In the middle ground, to the left of the previous episodes, Moses strikes the two shepherds who are trying to stop Jethro's daughters from watering their sheep. Then in the center foreground, he waters their flock (Exodus, 2:16f.); at the left, he cares for Jethro's flock and takes off his shoes because he is called by Jehovah. Farther on, he kneels before Jehovah, Who appears to him in the burning bush (Exodus, 3:1ff.). According to Horne and Schmarsow, the last episode shows Moses' return to Egypt with his family (Exodus, 4:19ff.), while others contend it shows the Exodus itself (Exodus, 14). The first thesis is preferable, since with Moses' return there would be a closer parallel to Christ's return to Galilee, followed by the miracle of the leper. Steinmann says that the fresco was also supposed to contain the Exodus and the crossing of the Red Sea, but after Sixtus IV defeated the Duke of Calabria on August 24, 1482, the Pope wanted to have the crossing painted separately to celebrate his victory and commissioned Piero di Cosimo to do it. Since the crossing was not included in Botticelli's frescoes, we could assume the date to be later than August 1482. But the assumption is not warranted, since we have evidence that Sandro was in Florence for the summer, or at least October 5. The fresco would have had to be painted in less than a month.

Plate 88

SCENES FROM THE LIFE OF MOSES. Detail: Jethro's daughters.

Plate 89

SCENES FROM THE LIFE OF MOSES. Detail of plate 88.

Plate 90

SCENES FROM THE LIFE OF MOSES. Detail: one of Moses' followers in the return to Egypt, at the extreme left.

Plate 91

SCENES FROM THE LIFE OF MOSES. Detail: one of Moses' followers, at the left by the tree.

Plate 92

TEMPTATION OF CHRIST. *Fresco, 345.5 × 555, second section of the right wall.* Generally entitled, from its principal episode, the *Healing of the Leper.* The *Temptation of Christ* is more descriptive, however, of its iconography and symbolic meaning, and certainly complements the analogous fresco of the *Scenes from the Life of Moses.* These trials prepare Christ for His mission of redemption and thus show the temptations: at the left, on the rock, the Devil, dressed as a pilgrim, asks Christ to turn stones into bread; at the center, near the temple, he defies Him to leap; at the right, Christ casts the Devil down, who is revealed beneath his robes, after the third temptation (the offer of the kingdoms), while the angels lay the banquet. The group with Christ, in the left middle ground, has been interpreted as Christ's return to Galilee after the temptations "by virtue of the Spirit" (the angels symbolizing the Spirit) according to Luke, 4:14. Others insist Christ is watching the leper's sacrifice from a distance. Steinmann explained the meaning of the main episode: the leper offers sacrifices after his cure, as described in Leviticus, 14. The Old Testament sacrifice was forcibly included among the trials of Christ in order to satisfy the Pope's desire to commemorate his works: the erection of the Hospital of Santo Spirito (the façade in the fresco), his loyalty as a Franciscan to the spirit of St Francis, who had treated the sick, symbolized by the leper, and his defense of the divinity of Christ's blood against the doubts raised by the Dominicans. Horne interprets the scene, however, according to Matthew, 8:4, where Christ tells the leper to go to the priest, one of His first miracles after the temptations. None the less, the commemoration of the Hospital of Santo Spirito was probably intended. Other interpretations have attempted to see analogies with the current political situation of the time, but they seem too ingenious.

Many of the personages in the foreground were apparently painted from life, and critics have tried to identify them. The old man with the cane, at the extreme right (plate 97), may have been Girolamo Riario, the nephew of Sixtus IV and Count of Forlí, who married Caterina Sforza in 1480 and became a marshal of the Church. Schmarsow thinks it was a certain Della Rovere, the palace chamberlain. The cardinal standing to the left of the woman with the firewood is probably Giuliano della Rovere, another of the Pope's nephews, who became Pope Julius II. Schmarsow and Gamba think it is Raffaello Riario, the cardinal who was saying Mass when Giuliano de' Medici was killed and his brother Lorenzo threatened by the Pazzi conspirators. The person standing behind the priest (plate 98) may have been the General of the Confraternity of the Holy Ghost (a Della Rovere) or Ferrante of Aragon, the King of Naples. The two large oak trees are generally interpreted as heraldic symbols of the Della Rovere ("of the oak" in Italian) family. Gamba detects a reminiscence of Leonardo da Vinci's *Adoration of the Magi* (1481) in the group seated in the left foreground.

Steinmann's claim that this is the first of three frescoes Botticelli painted is frequently repeated, but founded on his own erroneous dating of the *Scenes from the Life of Moses* and the *Punishment of Korah,* as autumn 1482 for the first, and winter 1483 for the second. In reality, no historical argument can apply here, and given the limited period in which they were completed, it would be unreasonable to attempt a dating on the basis of style. I have preferred arranging the frescoes according to their themes.

Plate 93

TEMPTATION OF CHRIST. Detail: upper right, Christ casts down the Devil.

Plate 94

TEMPTATION OF CHRIST. Detail: the center, the group at the left of the participants in the leper's sacrifice.

Plate 95

TEMPTATION OF CHRIST. Detail: lower right, the woman carrying firewood with the child carrying grapes.

Plate 96

TEMPTATION OF CHRIST. Detail: toward the lower right, the head of one of the churchmen, possibly Giuliano della Rovere or Raffaello Riario.

Plate 97

TEMPTATION OF CHRIST. Detail: the extreme right, below, the head of the supposed Girolamo Riario or the palace chamberlain.

Plate 98

TEMPTATION OF CHRIST. Central detail: the two participants in the leper's sacrifice (the second may be either the General of the Confraternity of the Holy Ghost, or Ferrante of Aragon).

Plate 99

TEMPTATION OF CHRIST. Detail: extreme right, head of a youth.

Plate 100

PUNISHMENT OF KORAH. *Fresco, 348.5 × 570, fifth section of the left wall.* Parallel in symbolic meaning to Perugino's *Delivery of the Keys,* located in front. The theme revolves around the rebels against Aaron who were punished by Moses. At the right, the rebels are warned by Moses, who is in danger of being stoned (Pastor's interpretation is untenable; that is, that Moses is turning over a rebel to his followers to be stoned). At the center, the trial by incense: Moses has Aaron and Eleazar on the one side, and the rebels on the other, burn incense. By a miracle, the smoke from the incense burned by the rebels turns on them, and proves Aaron's right to be priest. At the left, the rebels fall under Moses, while Aaron's two sons are lifted by clouds. Steinmann pointed out that the Pope was symbolically warning those who were reacting against his authority, with an allusion to the attempt by Andrew Zamometic, (an archbishop, and since 1478 Frederick III's Ambassador to Rome), to denounce and depose the Pope, whom he called the "Devil's son." His attempt was made in the spring of 1482 and he committed suicide in prison in 1484. There is probably a relationship between the fresco and Zamometic's *coup*, but references by contemporaries are not sufficient proof when the subject is so readily available from the Bible. To date the painting on this basis would be wrong, because documents show clearly that Botticelli was in Florence when Zamometic was arrested (December 21, 1482) and abjured (June 2, 1483). In fact the Pope had had difficulties with Zamometic earlier; we know that he sent a Legate to Germany in May 1482, to ask for the Archbishop's arrest. Thus, if the fresco was really related to these events, it could have been executed in the spring of 1482.

There are a number of portraits. Steinmann, and later, Gamba, see a self-portrait in the man facing us on the extreme right (plate 103), but other critics definitively reject the possibility. The young man in profile behind Moses, on the left, may have been Alessandro Farnese, the future Pope Paul II (plate 104), who is accompanied by his teacher, Pomponio Leto (plate 105). Other critics have advanced different identities.

The drawing in the Uffizi, numbered 146, traditionally ascribed to Botticelli, was attributed by Ulmann to Filippino and used to prove that the younger Lippi collaborated in the Roman frescoes. Horne considered it a copy, which Filippino did from memory, after his stay in Rome in 1489–93 to paint the frescoes in Santa Maria sopra Minerva. Gamba observes that several of the figures which are clothed in the fresco are nude in the drawing and concludes that the Uffizi drawing might have been a first sketch by Botticelli.

Plate 101

PUNISHMENT OF KORAH. Detail: the left, the port. (For the personages, see plates 104 and 105.)

Plate 102

PUNISHMENT OF KORAH. Detail: the right, the attempt to stone Moses.

Plate 103

PUNISHMENT OF KORAH. Detail: the extreme right, the so-called self-portrait of Botticelli.

Plate 104

PUNISHMENT OF KORAH. Detail: a head at the left, variously identified as a portrait of Alessandro Farnese, or of Raffaello Riario.

Plate 105

PUNISHMENT OF KORAH. Detail: a head at the left, variously identified as Pomponio Leto, as the Cardinal of Portugal, Giorgio Costa, or as the Apostolic Referee, Chierigati.

Plate 106

RESURRECTED CHRIST. *Panel, 44.5 × 29. Detroit, Institute of Arts.* It has been in various collections: Gavet in Paris, Belmont in Newport, and Valentiner in Detroit. Yashiro published it as an autograph Botticelli, datable around 1483–84, but he was supported only by Van Marle, who dated it around the time of the Sistine frescoes, by Berenson, and the editor of the catalog, *Duveen Pictures in Public Collections.* While other critics were silent about it, Mesnil said it was a workshop product, harder than a similar painting in Bergamo (see Part 4, plate 154). The calm vigor and the magnificent hands mark it as an authentic Botticelli, painted around the time of the Sistine frescoes and the *Adoration of the Magi* in Washington (plates 108–109). This Christ is unquestionably the archetype of two similar paintings in Bergamo and in Cambridge, Massachusetts, both school products painted almost fifteen years later in the master's late style.

Plate 107

PORTRAIT OF A LADY. *Panel, 48 × 35.5. London, Rothermere Collection.* Originally in the Trifulzio Collection in Milan. Berenson had ascribed it to "Sandro's friend" in 1899, ignored it in 1932 and called it a Botticelli in his edition of 1936. A. Venturi and Mesnil reject it while other critics are silent. L. Venturi accepts it, adding that it has been restored, and so does Van Marle, who dates the portrait with the *Portrait of a Young Woman* in the Pitti Palace (plate 51) in the artist's youthful period (1475–76). I think it is more likely a painting of the same period as the Roman frescoes, since the line has the broadness, and the chiaroscuro the density which characterize so many heads in the Sistine frescoes.

Plates 108–109

ADORATION OF THE MAGI. *Panel, 71 × 104. Washington, D.C., National Gallery.* Acquired in France from the engraver Perallis, who had, it seems, purchased it from a Roman collector, the panel went to the Hermitage in Petrograd as a Mantegna. Waagen recognized it there in 1864 as a Botticelli. In 1933, it was sold, and then acquired by the Mellon Collection in 1940. Generally identified as the same *Adoration of the Magi* cited in the *Anonimo Gaddiano* as among Botticelli's Roman works. The date would thus be around 1481–82. The oak tree might be considered a confirmation, since it was the symbol of the Pope's family, the Della Rovere. The painting was probably done around 1481–82, in Rome or in Florence after his return. Florence

may be justified if we note the influence of Leonardo's *Adoration of the Magi* (1481) in it, and especially in the broad landscape and in the solemn architecture, a hint of Perugino and Signorelli, both of whom Botticelli had met while painting his frescoes in the Sistine Chapel.

Plate 110

ADORATION OF THE MAGI. Detail: the center.

Plate 111

ADORATION OF THE MAGI. Detail: the right side.

Plate 112

ABUNDANCE. *Drawing, 31.7 × 25.3. London, British Museum. Black pencil, pen, wash and lead highlights on prepared reddish paper.* The drawing appeared in the Rogers Sale in 1856 as a Verrocchio; it then went to various collectors—Morris Moore, Robinson, Malcolm. Since Ulmann (1893), it has been universally attributed to Botticelli. Yashiro dates it around 1476. More frequently, with greater reason, it has been dated after the Roman period, around 1482. Also cf. Warburg (1932) and Kurz (1937–38).

Plate 113

PALLAS AND THE CENTAUR. *Canvas, 207 × 148. Florence, Uffizi Gallery.* Ridolfi published it in 1893, after he had found it hanging in one of the corridors of the Pitti Palace and transferred it to the royal apartments. It was taken to the Uffizi in 1922. Ridolfi thought the painting was the one mentioned by Vasari in Lorenzo the Elder's house; that is, painted for Lorenzo the Magnificent. But Vasari describes the *Pallas* as rising from a pyre, and so it cannot be the same painting. Horne showed from his research that like the *Primavera* and the *Birth of Venus*, this canvas belonged to the sons of

Pierfrancesco de' Medici. It is listed in the inventory made in 1516 in order to divide the Medici properties between Lorenzo's son, Pierfrancesco, and Giovanni's son, Giovanni dalle Bande Nere. The painting is listed in the inventories taken of the villa in Castello in 1598 and 1638, and must, therefore, have gone to Giovanni dalle Bande Nere. It was taken to the Pitti Palace in the nineteenth century. Bardi reproduced it with the title *Allegory*, ascribing it to Botticelli. Berenson dated the canvas between the *Primavera* (1477–78) and the *Birth of Venus* (a little after 1480). Horne thought it was painted around 1488 to commemorate the alliance between Lorenzo and Pope Innocent VIII. A. Venturi, Van Marle and Gamba date the painting immediately after the Roman period, about 1482–83, and I think this the most probable date (more towards 1482). Not only does the Centaur derive, as Tietze-Conrat has noted, from a Vatican sarcophagus, but the rock resembles a Roman ruin, and the plastic fullness of the figure, the breadth of the background, suggest Perugino and Signorelli,

whom Botticelli met in Rome. The subject has had a number of political interpretations (Lorenzo the Magnificent triumphs over the Neapolitan court intrigues, or over the Pazzi conspirators and other domestic enemies, or the figures are symbolic of his balanced government), but the moral allegory is more persuasive. Wittkower (1939) sees it as the reconciliation of wisdom and instinct in Lorenzo de' Medici (referred to by the design of the diamond rings on Pallas' dress). Gombrich (1945) identifies the Centaur as the human soul, made up of instinct and reason, joined by wisdom (Minerva-Mens). All according to the teachings of Ficino, who had remarked, "our beast is sense ... our man is reason."

Plate 114

PALLAS AND THE CENTAUR. Detail of the Centaur.

Plate 115

PALLAS AND THE CENTAUR. Detail: Pallas' head.

Color Plate III

PALLAS AND THE CENTAUR. Detail of plate 113.

THE FRESCOES IN THE TORNABUONI-LEMMI VILLA

Plates 116–124

The two frescoes which used to decorate the loggia of the Tornabuoni Villa (plates 116 and 117) in the Macerelli district, a former suburb, now part of Florence, were discovered under whitewash in 1873. In 1882, they were detached and sold to the Louvre. A third fresco remained at the villa because of its bad condition; we can barely make out a landscape and an old man dressed in red. The fresco was recognized as Botticelli's work by Conti (1881 and 1882) and Ephrussi (1882), followed

by Ridolfi (1890). The principal characters were identified as Lorenzo Tornabuoni, Giovanni's son, who was beheaded on August 17, 1497 for having participated in a conspiracy to restore Piero de' Medici, and Giovanna degli Albizi (who died very young in 1488) by comparing a medal cast by Niccolò Fiorentino. The fresco was painted on the occasion of their marriage on June 15, 1486 (according to Ammirato, 1642). The identifications were accepted, but Theime pointed out that the girl does not resemble

Giovanna degli Albizi at all. This evidence derives from the image on Niccolò Fiorentino's medal and from the well-known figure in Ghirlandaio's *Visitation* in the choir of Santa Maria Novella, which corresponds exactly to the medal and also to a panel that has been traditionally accepted as Giovanna's portrait by Ghirlandaio, now in the Pierpont Morgan Library in New York. The young girl in the fresco looks like the unknown young girl in the Ghirlandaio *Visitation* who is following Giovanna. Mesnil is the only critic to recognize the validity of Thieme's observation, and went on to note that the emblem next to the so-called Giovanna is not the Albizi family crest (concentric circles); the Albizi crest has been added in tempera to the other fresco (plate 116). We are confronted here with an addition made in 1486 at the time of the marriage, in order to change the frescoes to suit the occasion. Gombrich has even doubted that the Lemmi Villa was ever owned by Giovanni Tornabuoni. It follows then that the date of the two works should be estimated several years before 1486. A stylistic analysis confirms this: it is difficult to locate these compositions which are marked by a flowing, musical line between the *Madonna* in Berlin (Part 3, plate 20) and the *Madonna of the Pomegranate* (1487) where the line is tenser and we find some hints of languor. More appropriate certainly is a date closer to the Roman frescoes (1481–82), just before the *Birth of Venus* (Part 3, plates 12–13), which repeats in a more sentimental and easier tone the graceful feminine figures of the frescoes in the Tornabuoni-Lemmi Villa. We should say 1483 is the most probable date for this masterpiece.

Plate 116

LORENZO TORNABUONI (?) AND THE GRACES. *Detached fresco, 227 × 269.* Minerva leads the young man (in whom we could easily identify Lorenzo Tornabuoni, but he may be someone else in that very numerous family) before the Arts of the Trivium and Quadrivium, presided over by Rhetoric.

Plate 117

A LADY AND FOUR ALLEGORICAL FIGURES. *Fresco, 212 × 284.* The girl, mistakenly identified as Giovanna degli Albizi, could be a sister of Lorenzo Tornabuoni (otherwise not documented or cited by Sitta) or another young lady of the family. The old man dressed in red who can be seen in the fresco left on the wall could be Giovanni Tornabuoni.

Plate 118

LORENZO TORNABUONI (?) AND THE GRACES. Detail: the supposed Lorenzo.

Plate 119

LORENZO TORNABUONI (?) AND THE GRACES. Detail: Rhetoric.

Plate 120

LORENZO TORNABUONI (?) AND THE GRACES. Detail: one of the Liberal Arts.

Plate 121

A LADY AND FOUR ALLEGORICAL FIGURES. Detail: one of the Graces.

Plate 122

A LADY AND FOUR ALLEGORICAL FIGURES. Detail: another of the Graces.

Plate 123

A LADY AND FOUR ALLEGORICAL FIGURES. Detail: the young girl.

Plate 124

A LADY AND FOUR ALLEGORICAL FIGURES. Detail: Venus and one of the Graces.

PAINTINGS ATTRIBUTED TO BOTTICELLI

Plate 125

HAVEMAYER MADONNA. *Oval panel. New York, Metropolitan Museum of Art.* Once part of the Harnisch Collection in Philadelphia before being acquired by the Havemayer Collection. Originally in the Parish Church of Castelfranco di Sopra (Valdarno), it went to the chapel in Cerreto belonging to the Baglioni family, who sold it around 1900. Published as a work by Filippo Lippi by Colasanti (1903) and ascribed by L. Venturi to Lippi's school, the painting was attributed to Botticelli by Berenson in 1932, and by Gamba (1936), who considers it Botticelli's first known work. Mesnil (1938) doubts its authenticity, and most critics are silent on the matter. Since I have not seen the original, I cannot make an accurate judgment.

Plate 126

MADONNA AND CHILD WITH TWO ANGELS. *Panel. Manhasset, New York, Brady Collection.* The attribution is by Berenson, accepted by Gamba and Bettini. Mesnil explicitly rejects it, while other critics ignore it. I do not see the influences of Pesellino and Verocchio that Gamba claims are in the painting (while Bettini notes that such influences would have reached Sandro indirectly, through Lippi's frescoes in Prato). The composition is more elaborate than the *Havemayer Madonna* (plate 125) or the *Madonna and Child* of the Innocenti (plate 1). Therefore it must be later. Since I

have not seen the original, I would not make a positive statement, but I tend to think it autograph.

Plate 127

MADONNA ENTHRONED. *Fresco, 168 × 112. Florence-Settignano, Chapel of the Vannella.* We are compelled to list this fresco among works attributed to the master because it has been almost completely disfigured by restorations. Major critics attribute it to Botticelli. The type—the Virgin and the affectionate Child—is unquestionably related to Botticelli. The least restored parts of the faces have the qualities we associate with his youthful period, especially to the *Corsini Madonna* in Washington, D.C. (plate 11). Thus, if it is a genuine Botticelli, we should date it about 1468.

Plate 128

MADONNA AND CHILD WITH A BOY. *Panel, 83.7 × 59. Chicago, Max and Leola Epstein Collection.* The panel was put up for sale at Féral's in Paris in 1907, and was then sold by the Van Buren Collection in Amsterdam in 1925. A. Venturi published it and placed it chronologically near the *Madonna of the Eucharist* in Boston (plate 35), but we would date it later. Bode accepted the attribution but dated it near the *Guidi Madonna* in the Louvre (plate 4). Yashiro dated it around 1474, while Van Marle preferred 1470 and a little earlier. Gamba considers it a copy of the *Duveen Madonna* (plate 10). In comparison, however, the *Duveen Madonna* betrays the same frailness as the *Madonna of the Rose Arbor* in the Louvre (plate 8) and other youthful works. This *Madonna*, on the other hand, has fuller forms, signs of his later period. Most probably, we are dealing with a workshop copy executed a few years later.

Plate 129

MADONNA ENTHRONED. *Panel, Formerly at Wantage, Lockinge House, Thomas Lloyd Collection.* Sold in 1947, but the new owner is unknown. The Arundel Club published it in 1904-5 as Botticelli's work, but Berenson, Yashiro, A. Venturi and Gamba recognized it as a workshop copy, with variants, of the Virgin in the supposed *Convertite Altarpiece* in the Uffizi (plate 22). Quite beautiful and probably painted under the master's supervision.

Plate 130

THE HOLY TRINITY WITH ST JOHN THE BAPTIST AND MARY MAGDALEN. *Panel, 220 × 190. London University (Courtauld Institute Gallery), Viscount Lee of Fareham Collection, formerly at Richmond.* This panel belonged to Lord Winborne, and was acquired from the Monte di Pietà (a pawn bank) in Rome by Sir Henry Layard, on Morelli's advice. Yashiro not only published it as a Botticelli, but argued that it was the lost *Altarpiece of the Convertite* (cf. comment on plate 22), and related it to the incidents concerning the *Mary Magdalen* in Philadelphia (plates 26-29), which supposedly would be the predella of the *Altarpiece*. Most critics accept the hypothesis, but Mesnil has justifiably pointed out that the composition is unusual for Botticelli, with the figures of Tobias and the angel (otherwise very Botticellian) out of scale and the mediocre angels badly done. Berenson considers it was done "for the most part" by Botticelli. Scholars have not been able to agree on its dating: Yashiro dates it 1474 (the Verrocchio-Pollaiuolo moment), A. Venturi to the Roman visit, Bode 1490-95, while Gamba places it near the *Primavera*, that is, about 1478. Because he detects a touch of Andrea del Castagno's influence, Bettini would incline to 1478, but adds that there is a strong resemblance to the Verrocchio *Baptism* in the Uffizi, which would date it earlier. The uncertainties are probably due to the fact that this is a workshop product which combines elements from several periods. While Gamba insists there is a strong relationship between St John and the drawing in the Uffizi (Part 3, plate 23), in reality only the pose is similar. The sheet appears clearly to belong to a later phase, nearer the *St Barnabas Altarpiece* (Part 3, plate 29). Gamba assumes the panel was originally taller and arched, but that would not mitigate the unpleasantness of the work which makes it so dubious.

Plate 131

PORTRAIT OF A YOUNG MAN. *Panel. Heemstede, Haarlem, Von Gutmann Collection.* This came from the Von Nemes Collection in Budapest around 1930, by way of Kleinberger, the antiques firm. It was published as a Botticelli by H. Uhde-Bernays and A. Venturi, and accepted by Van Marle. Berenson only cites it in passing (*Dedalo*, 1932) as "authoritatively attributed to Botticelli," in order to illustrate the Botticellianism of the "Master of San Miniato"— but then he omits it from the index. The weakness in the glance, and a certain mechanical quality about the curly hair, make the attribution doubtful.

Plate 132

PORTRAIT OF A BOY. *Panel, 43 × 29. Besançon, Musée des Beaux-Arts.* Bears the inscription "el tempo consuma" (time wears). Attributed long ago to Masaccio and Verrocchio, it was ascribed to Botticelli by Berenson and Mesnil. But the painting has been variously attributed: Verrocchio or Botticini, Pollaiuolo's school, Piero del Pollaiuolo, non-Florentine, and Antonio del Pollaiuolo, a youthful work (says Ragghianti, 1949). Laclotte thinks it was painted by the same artist who painted the *Portrait of a Young Man* in the Rijksmuseum in Amsterdam, which in turn has been ascribed to Filippino or to Pollaiuolo. It should be excluded, in any case, from the Botticelli *œuvre*.

Plate 133a

PORTRAIT OF A YOUNG MAN. *Panel. New York, Metropolitan Museum of Art.* Formerly in the Friedsam Collection. Van Marle published it as a Botticelli, dating to about 1470–72, and Berenson included it in his catalog. The work of an imitator, someone in the Sellaio-Garbo circle.

Plate 133b

PORTRAIT OF A YOUNG MAN. *Panel. Naples, Museo Filangieri.* The painting used to carry Botticelli's name, but Kroeber rejected the attribution (1911), claiming it for no apparent reason as a Piero di Cosimo. Van Marle also rejected it, but considered it more reasonably as a copy of the similar subject in the Pitti (plate 19).

Color Plate IV

PALLAS AND THE CENTAUR. Detail of plate 113.

Plate 134a

PORTRAIT OF A YOUTH. *Panel, 41 × 31. Berlin, Staatliche Museen.* Acquired in 1829 on Rumohr's advice, it bore an attribution to Filippino Lippi until Morelli reascribed it (1886) to Raffaellino del Garbo. Ulmann considered a follower of Botticelli or of Filippino (someone, moreover, influenced by Perugino) as a likelier artist, and related the painting to the frescoes in San Martino de' Buonomini, but A. Venturi rejected the idea. Bode, however, ascribed it to Sandro, dating it within the five-year period from 1480 to 1485. Most critics have been reserved in their judgments, but the name Raffaellino del Garbo appears frequently (Berenson, Bodmer, Neilson, Berti and Baldini), and we are inclined to agree with this attribution.

Plate 134b

PORTRAIT OF A YOUTH. *Panel. Formerly in Zürich, Abels Collection.* Bode published it (1926) as a work dating from the same period as the Filangieri portrait (plate 133b), which he dates, in turn, to 1475. Van Marle is the only critic to accept the attribution; the others have remained noncommittal.

Plate 135

ANGEL OF THE ANNUNCIATION. *Drawing, 23.4 × 14.2. Florence, Uffizi Gallery. Silverpoint, lead and sepia on prepared paper.* Yashiro ascribed it to Botticelli, dating it 1474, but only Van Marle has seconded the attribution, dating it to the Roman period. It is not by Botticelli, but perhaps in the direction of Lorenzo di Credi.

Plate 136

HEAD OF AN ANGEL. *Drawing, 20 × 17. Rennes, Musée des Beaux-Arts.*

Silverpoint with lead highlights on prepared paper. The collection carries it as a Piero del Pollaiuolo, but Ragghianti (1938) holds that it is Botticelli's work, around the time of the *Fortitude*. Bertini agrees (1953). Closer to Piero del Pollaiuolo.

Plate 137

PORTRAIT OF A YOUNG MAN. *Panel, 51.5 × 35. London, National Gallery.* Acquired in 1916 from the Layard Collection in Venice, which in turn bought it from the Arrigoni family in Bergamo around 1865. In the nineteenth century, the work was variously ascribed to Dürer, Foppa and Signorelli. The attribution to Botticelli was made in the London catalog in 1929, and Berenson and Vertova accepted it. But most of the critics, including Holmes, Van Marle, Scharf, Neilson and Davies, have taken into account the information Morelli gave Layard when he acquired it, later supported by Frizzoni. They argue, and I think rightly, that the work should be ascribed to Raffaellino del Garbo.

Plate 138

PORTRAIT OF A YOUNG MAN. *Panel, 40.64 × 30.5. Philadelphia, Johnson Collection.* Berenson attributed the panel to "Sandro's friend," and Perkins published it as such in 1905, identifying the subject as Giuliano de' Medici. Bode, however, ascribed it to the master and dated it near the *Portrait of a Man with a Medal* in the Uffizi (plate 47). Berenson then (1932) accepted it as a youthful work. Most of the critics have been silent about it, but Kroeber and Van Marle have rejected it. Although there are many elements related to the artist's Pollaiuolo phase, a certain heavyhandedness leads us to think it is a pupil's effort.

Plate 139

MADONNA AND CHILD WITH ANGELS. *Panel, 79 × 55. Paris, Louvre.* Reinach (*Répertoire*, I), followed by A. Venturi, assigned it to Botticelli's school. Logan, in 1900, had attributed it to Jacopo del Sellaio, and Van Marle to "Sandro's friend." But the affinities to Botticelli's early works are greater than in anything Sellaio did, with the result that Berenson was led to consider it a copy of Sellaio done by Botticelli. We prefer to accept the opinion of Gamba, Mesnil, Berti and Baldini, that the work was produced jointly by Botticelli and Filippino around 1473–75.

Plate 140

POMONA. *Canvas, 192 × 105. Chantilly, Musée Condé.* The older ascription to Mantegna was corrected in 1864 by Cavalcaselle, who saw the painting in the Reiset Collection in France, which had acquired it in Rome. But Ulmann considered it a school product because of the derivations from the *Abundance* in the British Museum (plate 112). Berenson thought it was by the same artist who did the *tondo* in the Borghese Gallery (Part 4, plate 144); Horne agreed and even claimed the figure was derived from the woman carrying firewood in the *Scenes from the Life of Moses* (plate 95). Van Marle numbered it among his own "Master of the Gothic Buildings" works. Several critics agree it is a workshop product. A well-executed work, no doubt, by the *bottega*; in fact by the same follower who did the Roman *tondo*.

Plate 141

THE STORY OF NASTAGIO DEGLI ONESTI, FIRST EPISODE. *Panel, 84 × 142. Barcelona, Cambó Collection.* Part of a series of three panels for chairbacks illustrating Boccaccio's *novella* about Nastagio degli Onesti. Here, on the left in the middle ground, Nastagio sets up his tent in the pine wood of Ravenna to seek solace for his unhappy love for the daughter of Paolo Traversari. He wanders disconsolately through the wood (left foreground), when he sees the woman pursued by Guido degli Anastagi and seized by the hound (right and center foreground). He attempts to defend her but in vain. Vasari remembers the panels (as Botticelli's work) in the Pucci house, where they were kept until 1868. They were sold to the Barker Collection of London (Milanesi, 1879) and then to the Leyland Collection. In 1892, the Aynard Collection of Lyons acquired them and shortly after ceded three of them to the Spiridon in Paris, from which they were acquired by the present owners. The fourth went to the Donaldson Collection, from which it passed to the Watney Collection in Charlbury. Since the last two panels bear the Pucci and Medici crests on the left, and the Pucci and Bini crests on the right, the commentators who wrote for the Le Monnier edition of Vasari (1846, V) hazarded that the panels had been painted for the wedding of Pierfrancesco Bini with Lucrezia Pucci in 1487. But Horne noticed that according to heraldic rules, the position of the crests indicated that a Pucci married one of the Bini women; he therefore associated the panels with the marriage of Giannozzo Pucci and Lucrezia Bini in 1483. Horne's assumption has been generally accepted, except by Berenson. Beginning with Richte and Ulmann, criticism has considered the panels as workshop products conceived by Botticelli but carried out principally by Jacopo del

Sellaio or, more probably, Bartolomeo di Giovanni.

Plate 142

THE STORY OF NASTAGIO DEGLI ONESTI, SECOND EPISODE. *Panel, 84 × 112. Barcelona, Cambó Collection.* Nastagio watches the vision in horror. Guido removes the woman's vitals and feeds them to the dogs, center foreground. The woman awakes and the chase begins again (center background).

Plate 143

THE STORY OF NASTAGIO DEGLI ONESTI, THIRD EPISODE. *Panel, 84 × 112. Barcelona, Cambó Collection.* Nastagio asks the Traversari family to come to the wood for a banquet and they see the vision.

Plate 144

THE STORY OF NASTAGIO DEGLI ONESTI, FOURTH EPISODE. *Panel, 84 × 112. Charlbury, Watney Collection.* Warned by the vision, the girl consents to the marriage, and the wedding feast is celebrated.

Plate 145

PORTRAIT OF A YOUNG MAN. *Panel, 54 × 40. Paris, Louvre.* From the Pillet Collection in Paris in 1882, where it was carried as a portrait of "Burchiello" by Filippino Lippi. Ulmann ascribed it (1893) to Botticelli, dating it between 1470 and 1478. Berenson thought it by "Sandro's friend," and Van Marle agreed. Although sometimes attributed to his school, the portrait has been identified as Botticelli's work by Bode, Schmarsow, Yashiro and Mesnil. Gamba dates it around 1478 and thinks Filippino collaborated. Baldini and Berti recently seconded his opinion. The unquestionable Botticellian aspect of this painting is mitigated by a minuteness and surface nervousness characteristic of Filippino. He may have done the painting after a drawing by the master while he worked in his shop, probably around 1478.

Plates 146–148

DOOR OF THE SALA DEGLI ANGELI. *Intarsias, Urbino, Ducal Palace.* The drawing for these intarsias, especially for the upper panels showing *Apollo* (plate 147) and *Pallas* (plate 148) and measuring 157 × 67 and 158 × 69, was first attributed jointly to Botticelli and Piero della Francesca by Calzini (1899), but the attribution to Botticelli was not accepted then, and so Budinich ascribed its conception to Baccio Pontelli, who was probably the carver. L. Venturi ascribed the conception to Francesco di Giorgio for the most part. Longhi, Gamba, Arcangeli and Salmi have reascribed it to Botticelli—and Salmi has even ascribed the idea for the lower panels to him. The date inscribed on the ceiling of the study, 1476, is a precise indication of when Botticelli furnished these designs, during a time when he was still quite influenced by Pollaiuolo.

Plates 149–151

STUDY OF FEDERICO DA MONTEFELTRO. *Intarsias, Urbino, Ducal Palace.* See comment on plates 146–148. The figures are: *Charity* (93 × 48) and *Hope* (97 × 43), plate 149; *Faith* (97 × 41) and *Duke Frederick* (99 × 50), plate 150; and a still life, plate 151.

MADONNA AND CHILD. *Fragment of a panel, 45 × 32. New York, Blumenthal Collection.* Formerly in the Butler Collection in London and the Hainauer Collection in Berlin. Berenson ascribed the fragment to the young Botticelli in 1932, thus correcting his earlier ascription to Pierfrancesco Fiorentino. Variously attributed to Lippi, Lippi's school, to Zanobi Machiavelli and to Giovanni di Francesco. Ragghianti's attribution to Giovanni di Francesco cannot be accepted because the painting obviously depends on Lippi's *Madonna* in Munich, which was painted around 1465; that is, after Giovanni's death. The painting is not by Botticelli either, as it has none of the transformations he wrought on Lippi's forms. (Cf. Pittaluga, 1949.)

DEPOSITION. *Panel, 93 × 64. Cherbourg, Musée.* Previously in the Thomas Henry Collection. Berenson suggested that the young Botticelli painted this, after he had cataloged it as a Filippo Lippi, following Reinach, who was the first to publish it (*Répertoire*, III, 1929). Generally, and justifiably, this beautiful work is attributed to Lippi (cf. Pittaluga, 1949 and Laclotte, 1956, etc.).

MADONNA AND CHILD WITH ST JOHN THE BAPTIST. *Panel, 89 × 68. Formerly in Munich, the Nemès Collection.* In 1837, this went from Cardinal Fesch's Collection to the Spiridon Collection in Paris. In 1929, it was acquired by the Munich Collection, the last location we know of. The Spiridon Collection ascribed the painting to Verrocchio, but Fischel related it to the series of *Madonnas* Botticelli did as a young man and claimed it was more Botticellian than the panels in the Hospital of the Innocenti (plate 1), in the Accademia (plate 6) and in Naples (plate 12b). Van Marle accepted the Fischel proposal with some doubts, while L. Venturi ascribed the painting to Filippo Lippi. Mesnil turned down the Botticelli attribution, and said it was by Verrocchio's *bottega*. Pittaluga's suggestion seems the most plausible, that it was painted by the artist who painted the *Nativity* (No. 1343 in the Louvre) and the *Virgin and Saints* (No. 60 in the Budapest Museum)—a painter in Lippi's style, who was influenced by Verrocchio and Pesellino. Perhaps the *Madonna* in Marseilles, frequently attributed to Botticelli, is by the same anonymous artist.

MADONNA AND CHILD. *Panel. Marseilles, Musée des Beaux-Arts.* Put on exhibition as a Botticelli, the painting was excluded by Bode. A. Venturi judged it a school product. Van Marle assigned it to "Sandro's friend." A very Verrocchian work, perhaps ascribable to the artist who painted the *Nativity* (No. 1343 in the Louvre; see preceding comment).

BAPTISM OF CHRIST. *Panel, 177 × 151. Florence, Uffizi Gallery.* According to Ragghianti, this is Botticelli's work rather than Verrocchio's, except for the well-known part by Leonardo. Ragghianti makes his judgment despite the uncertainty of the information the sources provide, and even doubts the existence of a painter called Verrocchio. Thus the series of *Madonnas* attributed to Verrocchio would represent an unclear phase of Botticelli's youthful work. But the comparisons he makes with the supposed *Altarpiece of the Convertite* in the Uffizi (plate 22) and with the *Guidi Baptism* (which is not by Botticelli, and reflects, in any case, his late style) only reveal radical differences in style. Therefore, even if it has not been proved that Verrocchio really did the group (the *Baptism*, the *Madonna* in Berlin, the London *Madonna*) in question, it

cannot be included in the Botticelli catalog.

ASSUMPTION OF THE VIRGIN. *Panel, 228.5 × 377. London, National Gallery.* According to Vasari, Botticelli painted this on a subject provided by Matteo Palmieri for his chapel in San Pier Maggiore, where it remained until the church was demolished in 1783. The painting was transferred to the Palmieri house. Sold in the early nineteenth century, it was acquired by the National Gallery in 1882 from the Hamilton Collection. Vasari notes that the painting was accused of being heretical, and, in fact, it shows the unorthodox theory Palmieri wrote about in his *Città di Vita* (published posthumously and immediately condemned as heretical). According to Palmieri, men's souls are the angels who remained neutral during Lucifer's rebellion. Cavalcaselle attributed the panel to Botticelli, but Bode associated it with works by Botticini, to whom it is generally ascribed today. Davies, on external evidence, argues convincingly that Botticini probably painted it around 1474–76.

PORTRAIT OF A YOUNG MAN. *Panel, 55 × 40.7. Edinburgh, National Gallery of Scotland.* Bodkins published it as autograph and dated it a little after 1480. The analogous painting in the Louvre (plate 145) supposedly derives from it (cf. Stanley Cursitor, in *Apollo*, 1933). But here we have a weak copy of the Louvre panel (Scharf, Mesnil, etc.).

PORTRAIT OF A YOUNG MAN. *Round panel, diameter 37. Stockholm, Royal Collection.* Sirén assigned it to Botticelli and identified the sitter as Lorenzo Tornabuoni. Berenson ascribed it to Botticini, seconded by Khünel, Kroeber, and L. Collobi

Ragghianti. Van Marle unconvincingly attributes it to Lorenzo di Credi.

THE LEGEND OF ST ANDREW. *Panel, 25 × 50. Liverpool, Walker Art Gallery.* A part of a predella, cataloged in the Roscoe Collection Sale (1816) as a work by Andrea del Castagno, along with a *Martyrdom of St Sebastian* of the same size. Fry ascribed it to Botticelli (1930) and referred to Kenneth Clark's opinion. But Berenson rightly ascribed both paintings to Bartolomeo di Giovanni (Domenico's student), and his attribution has been generally accepted. (Cf. *Liverpool Bulletin,* October 1954.)

LOCATION OF PAINTINGS

AJACCIO
MUSÉE FESCH
Madonna and Child with Angel
(plate 2).

ALTENBURG (GERMANY)
LINDENAU MUSEUM
Portrait of a Woman as St Catherine
(plate 37).

BARCELONA
CAMBÓ COLLECTION
*Story of Nastagio degli Onesti, First
Episode* (plate 141; attribution)
*Story of Nastagio degli Onesti, Second
Episode* (plate 142; attribution).
*Story of Nastagio degli Onesti, Third
Episode* (plate 143; attribution).

BERGAMO
ACCADEMIA CARRARA
Portrait of Giuliano de' Medici
(plate 49a).

BERLIN
STAATLICHE MUSEEN
St Sebastian (plate 45).
Portrait of Giuliano de' Medici
(plate 49b).
Raczinsky Tondo (plate 63).
Portrait of a Young Man (plate 134a;
attribution).

BESANÇON
MUSÉE DES BEAUX-ARTS
Portrait of a Boy (plate 132; attri-
bution).

BOSTON
ISABELLA STEWART GARDNER
MUSEUM
Madonna of the Eucharist (plate 35).

CHANTILLY
MUSÉE CONDÉ
Pomona (plate 140; attribution).

CHARLBURY (ENGLAND)
WATNEY COLLECTION
*Story of Nastagio degli Onesti, Fourth
Episode* (plate 144; attribution).

CHERBOURG
MUSÉE DE PEINTURE
Deposition (see p. 80, "Attributed
Paintings").

CHICAGO
EPSTEIN COLLECTION
Madonna and Child with a Boy (plate
128; attribution).

DETROIT
INSTITUTE OF ARTS
Resurrected Christ (plate 106).

EDINBURGH
NATIONAL GALLERY OF SCOT-
LAND
Portrait of a Young Man (see p. 81,
"Attributed Paintings").

FLORENCE
ACCADEMIA
*Madonna and Child with St John the
Baptist* (plates 6–7).
Madonna of the Sea (plate 62).

BELVEDERE
San Martino Annunciation (plates 80–81).

CHURCH OF THE ANNUNZIATA
Madonna and Child (plate 30).

CHURCH OF OGNISSANTI
St Augustine (plates 78–79).

CHURCH OF SANTA MARIA NOVELLA
The Nativity (plate 59).

MUSEO DELL'OSPEDALE DEGLI INNOCENTI
Madonna and Child (plate 1).

PITTI PALACE
Portrait of a Young Man (plate 19).
Portrait of a Young Woman (plate 51).

UFFIZI GALLERY
Madonna of the Loggia (plate 3).
Madonna in Glory with Seraphim (plate 15).
Madonna of the Rose Arbor (plates 16–17).
Fortitude (plates 20–21).
Altarpiece of the Convertite (?) (plates 22–25).
Discovery of the Murder of Holofernes (plate 43).
Judith with the Head of Holofernes (plate 44).
Portrait of a Man with a Medal (plate 47).
Adoration of the Magi (plates 52–57).
Three Angels (drawing, plate 58).
Primavera (plates 64–77).
Pallas and the Centaur (plates 113–115).
Angel of the Annunciation (drawing, plate 135; attribution).
Baptism of Christ (see p. 81, "Attributed Paintings").

FLORENCE-
SETTIGNANO
CHAPEL OF THE VANNELLA

Madonna Enthroned (plate 127; attribution).

GLENS FALLS
(NEW YORK)
HYDE COLLECTION
Annunciation (plate 31).

HEEMSTEDE
(HAARLEM)
VON GUTMANN COLLECTION
Portrait of a Youth (plate 131; attribution).

LIVERPOOL
WALKER ART GALLERY
The Legend of St Andrew (see p. 82, "Attributed Paintings").

LONDON
BRITISH MUSEUM
Head of a Youth (see comment on plate 8).
Abundance (drawing, plate 112).

NATIONAL GALLERY
Madonna and Child (plate 12a).
Madonna and Child with Angels (plate 13b).
Adoration of the Magi (plates 32–34).
Tondo of the Adoration of the Magi (plates 38–42).
Portrait of a Young Man (plate 137; attribution).
Assumption of the Virgin (see p. 81, "Attributed Paintings").

ROTHERMERE COLLECTION
Portrait of a Lady (plate 107).

UNIVERSITY: LEE OF FAREHAM COLLECTION (Courtauld Institute Gallery)
The Holy Trinity with St John the Baptist and Mary Magdalen (plate 130; attribution).

VICTORIA AND ALBERT MUSEUM

Portrait of Esmeralda Bandinelli (?) (plate 36).

MANHASSET (NEW YORK)

BRADY COLLECTION

Madonna and Child with Angels (plate 126; attribution).

MARSEILLES

MUSÉE DES BEAUX-ARTS

Madonna and Child (see p. 81, "Attributed Paintings").

MILAN

CRESPI COLLECTION

Portrait of Giuliano de' Medici (plate 48b).

NAPLES

MUSEO FILANGIERI

Portrait of a Young Man (plate 133b; attribution).

NATIONAL GALLERIES OF CAPODIMONTE

Madonna and Child with Angels (plate 12b).

NEW YORK

BLUMENTHAL COLLECTION

Madonna and Child, fragment (see p. 80, "Attributed Paintings").

DUVEEN COLLECTION

Madonna and Child with Youth (plate 10).

METROPOLITAN MUSEUM OF ART

Havemayer Madonna (plate 125; attribution).
Portrait of a Young Man (plate 133a; attribution).

PARIS

LOUVRE

Guidi Madonna (plate 4).
Madonna and Child (plate 5).
Madonna and Child with St John (plates 8–9).
Madonna and Child with Angels (plate 14).
Lorenzo Tornabuoni [?] *and the Graces* (plates 116, 118–120).
A Lady and four Allegorical Figures (plates 117, 121–124).
Madonna and Child with Angels (plate 139; attribution).
Portrait of a Young Man (plate 145; attribution).

PHILADELPHIA

JOHN G. JOHNSON ART COLLECTION

Christ Teaching (plate 26).
Feast in the House of Simon (plate 27).
"Noli me tangere" (plate 28).
Last Moments of Mary Magdalen (plate 29).
Portrait of a Young Man (plate 138; attribution).

PIACENZA

MUSEO CIVICO

Madonna and Child with St John the Baptist (plate 83).

RENNES (FRANCE)

MUSÉE DES BEAUX-ARTS

Head of an Angel (drawing, plate 136).

SANTA MONICA (CALIFORNIA)

BARBARA HUTTON COLLECTION

Portrait of a Young Man (plate 18).

STOCKHOLM

ROYAL COLLECTION

Portrait of a Young Man (see pp. 81–82, "Attributed Paintings").

STRASBOURG

MUSÉE DES BEAUX-ARTS

Madonna and Child with Angels
(plate 13a).

URBINO

DUCAL PALACE

Intarsias of the Door of the Sala degli Angeli (plates 146–151; attribution).

VATICAN CITY

SISTINE CHAPEL

Pope St Evaristus (plate 84a).
Pope St Cornelius (plate 84b).
Pope St Sixtus (plate 85a).
Pope St Marcellinus (plate 85b).
Pope St Stephen (plate 86a).
Pope St Soter (plate 86b).
Pope St Lucius (plate 86c).
Scenes from the Life of Moses (plates 87–91).
Temptation of Christ (plates 92–99).
Punishment of Korah (plates 100–105).

WASHINGTON, D.C.

NATIONAL GALLERY OF ART

Madonna and Child (plate 11).

Portrait of Giuliano de' Medici (plate 50).
Portrait of a Youth (plate 60).
Adoration of the Magi (plates 108–111).

ZÜRICH

ALEGG STOCKAR COLLECTION

St Thomas Aquinas (plate 82).

LOCATION UNKNOWN

Portrait of a Medici, formerly in Florence, Corsini Gallery (plate 46).
Portrait of Lorenzo the Magnificent, formerly in Paris, Lazzaroni Collection (plate 48a).
Madonna Enthroned, formerly in Wantage, England, Lloyd Collection (plate 129; attribution).
Portrait of a Youth, formerly in Zürich, Abels Collection (plate 134b; attribution).
Madonna and Child with St John the Baptist, formerly in Munich, Nemès Collection (see pp. 80–81, "Attributed Paintings").

DESTROYED

Portrait of a Man, formerly in Naples, Museo Filangieri (plate 61).

REPRODUCTIONS

ACKNOWLEDGMENT FOR PLATES

B. *Anderson, Rome:* plates 1, 6, 11, 12b, 16, 19, 20, 43, 47, 49a, 51, 53–55, 61, 64–65, 66, 72–73, 75, 83–92, 94–99, 102–105, 107, 133b, 146–148, 150b. *Alinari, Florence:* 3, 7–9, 14–15, 17, 21, 46, 57, 59, 68–69, 71, 74, 93, 100–101, 116–124, 132, 139, 145. *Gabinetto Fotografico della Sovrintendenza alle Gallerie, Florence:* 22–25, 30, 44, 52, 58, 62, 78, 80–81b, 113–115, 127, 135. *Brogi, Florence:* 67, 70, 76, 77, 79. *Duveen Brothers, New York:* 10, 18. *National Gallery, London:* 12a, 13b, 32–33, 34, 38–42, 137. *Johnson Collection, Philadelphia:* 26–29, 138. *Walter Steinkopf, Berlin-Dahlem:* 45, 49b, 63. *National Gallery of Art, Washington, D.C.:* 50, 60, 108–111. *A. y. R. Mas, Barcelona:* 141–143. *Bulloz, Paris:* 2. *Archives Photographiques des Monuments Historiques de France, Paris:* 4. *Jean-Pierre Sudre, Paris:* 5. *George Philip Sauter, Glens Falls, New York:* 31. *Gardner Museum, Boston:* 35. *Victoria and Albert Museum, London:* 36. *Kunsthistorisches Institut, Leipzig:* 37. *A. Reali, Florence:* 56. *Institute of Art, Detroit:* 106. *British Museum, London:* 112. *Art Institute, Chicago:* 128. *Metropolitan Museum of Art, New York:* 133a. *Bildarchiv Foto, Marburg:* 134a. *Musée des Beaux-Arts, Rennes:* 136. The other illustrations are taken from the author's own files.

Material for all color plates was supplied by Scala, Florence.

Plate 62. MADONNA OF THE SEA Florence, Accademia

Plate 63. RACZINSKY TONDO Berlin, Staaliche Museen

Plates 64–65. PRIMA

Plate 66. *Detail of plates 64–65*

Plate 67. *Detail of plates 64–65*

Plate 68. *Detail of plates 64–65*

PRIMAVERA
Florence, Uffizi Gallery
(*detail of plates 64–65*)

Plate 69. *Detail of plates 64–65*

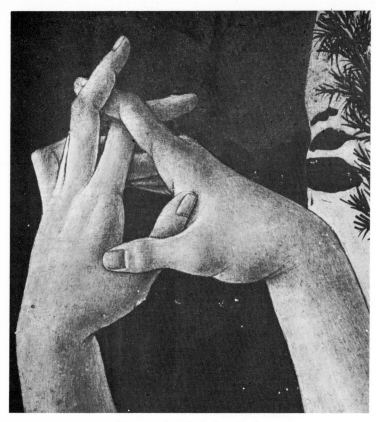

Plate 70. *Detail of plates 64–65*

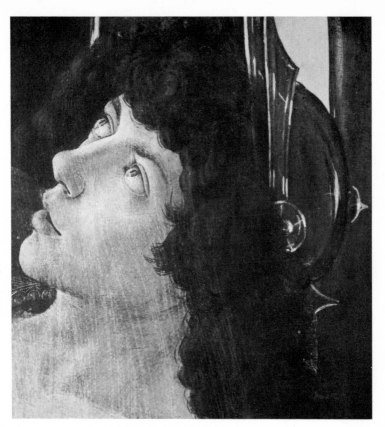

Plate 71. *Detail of plates 64–65*

Plate 72. *Detail of plates 64–65*

Plate 73. *Detail of plates 64–65*

Plate 74. *Detail of plates 64–65*

Plate 75. *Detail of plates 64–65*

Plate 76. *Detail of plates 64–65*

Plate 77. *Detail of plates 64–65*

Plate 78. ST AUGUSTINE Florence, Church of Ognissanti

Plate 79. *Detail of plate 78*

Plate 80. SAN MARTINO ANNUNCIATION Florence, Belvedere

Plate 81. *Detail of plate 80*

Plate 82. ST THOMAS AQUINAS Zürich, Alegg Stockar Collection

Plate 83. MADONNA AND CHILD WITH ST JOHN THE BAPTIST
Piacenza Museo Civico

Plate 84. POPE ST EVARISTUS and POPE ST CORNELIUS Vatican City,
Sistine Chapel

PRIMAVERA
Florence, Uffizi Gallery
(*detail of plates 64–65*)

Plate 85. POPE ST SIXTUS and POPE ST MARCELLINUS Vatican City,
Sistine Chapel

Plate 86. SS., POPES, STEPHEN, SOTER and LUCIUS Vatican City,
Sistine Chapel

Plate 87. SCENES FROM THE LIFE OF MOSES Vatican City, Sistine Chapel

Plate 88. *Detail of plate 87*

Plate 89. *Detail of plate 87*

Plate 90. *Detail of plate 87*

Plate 91. *Detail of plate 87*

Plate 92. TEMPTATION OF CHRIST Vatican City, Sistine Chapel

Plate 93. *Detail of plate 92*

Plate 94. *Detail of plate 92*

Plate 95. *Detail of plate 92*

Plate 96. *Detail of plate 92*

Plate 97. *Detail of plate 92*

Plate 98. *Detail of plate 92*

Plate 99. *Detail of plate 92*

Plate 100. PUNISHMENT OF KORAH Vatican City, Sistine Chapel

Plate 101. *Detail of plate 100*

Plate 102. *Detail of plate 100*

Plate 103. *Detail of plate 100*

Plate 104. *Detail of plate 100*

Plate 105. *Detail of plate 100*

Plate 106. RESURRECTED CHRIST Detroit, Institute of Arts

Plate 107. PORTRAIT OF A LADY London, Rothermere Collection

Plates 108–109. ADORATIO
Nati

THE MAGI Washington, D.C.,
Gallery

Plate 110. *Detail of plates 108–109*

Plate III. *Detail of plates 108–109*

Plate 112. ABUNDANCE London, British Museum

Plate 113. PALLAS AND THE CENTAUR Florence, Uffizi Gallery

Plate 114. *Detail of plate 113*

Plate 115. *Detail of plate 113*

Plate 116. LORENZO TORNABUONI (?) AND THE GRACES Paris, Louvre

PALLAS AND THE CENTAUR
Florence, Uffizi Gallery
(*detail of plate 113*)

Plate 117. A LADY AND FOUR ALLEGORICAL FIGURES Paris, Louvre

Plate 118. *Detail of plate 116*

Plate 119. *Detail of plate 116*

Plate 120. *Detail of plate 116*

Plate 121. *Detail of plate 117*

Plate 122. *Detail of plate 117*

Plate 123. *Detail of plate 117*

Plate 124. *Detail of plate 117*

ATTRIBUTED WORKS

Plate 125. HAVEMAYER MADONNA New York, Metropolitan Museum of Art (*attr.*)

Plate 126. MADONNA AND CHILD WITH ANGELS Long Island,
Brady Collection (*attr.*)

Plate 127. MADONNA ENTHRONED Florence-Settignano, Chapel of the
Vannella (*attr.*)

Plate 128. MADONNA AND CHILD WITH A BOY Chicago, Max and Leola
Epstein Collection (*attr.*)

Plate 129. MADONNA ENTHRONED formerly at Wantage, Lockinge
House, Thomas Lloyd Collection (*attr.*)

Plate 130. THE HOLY TRINITY WITH ST JOHN THE BAPTIST AND
MARY MAGDALEN London, University (Courtauld Institute Gallery),
Viscount Lee of Fareham Collection (*attr.*)

Plate 131. PORTRAIT OF A YOUNG MAN Heemstede, Haarlem, Von
Gutmann Collection (*attr.*)

Plate 132. PORTRAIT OF A BOY Besançon, Musée des Beaux-Arts (*attr.*)

Plate 133. PORTRAIT OF A YOUNG MAN New York, Metropolitan
Museum of Art (*attr.*) and Naples, Museo Filangieri (*attr.*)

Plate 134. PORTRAIT OF A YOUTH Berlin, Staatliche Museen (*attr.*) and formerly in Zürich, Abels Collection (*attr.*)

Plate 135. ANGEL OF THE ANNUNCIATION Florence, Uffizi Gallery
(attr.)

PALLAS AND THE CENTAUR
Florence, Uffizi Gallery
(*detail of plate 113*)

Plate 136. HEAD OF AN ANGEL Rennes, Musée des Beaux-Arts (*attr.*)

Plate 137. PORTRAIT OF A YOUNG MAN London, National Gallery
(*attr.*)

Plate 138. PORTRAIT OF A YOUNG MAN Philadelphia, Johnson Collection
(*attr.*)

Plate 139. MADONNA AND CHILD WITH ANGELS Paris, Louvre (*attr.*)

Plate 140. POMONA Chantilly, Musée Condé (*attr.*)

Plate 141. THE STORY OF NASTAGIO DEGLI ONESTI, FIRST EPISODE
Barcelona, Cambó Collection (*attr.*)

Plate 142. THE STORY OF NASTAGIO DEGLI ONESTI, SECOND
EPISODE Barcelona, Cambó Collection (*attr.*)

Plate 143: THE STORY OF NASTAGIO DEGLI ONESTI, THIRD EPISODE
Barcelona, Cambó Collection (*attr.*)

Plate 144. THE STORY OF NASTAGIO DEGLI ONESTI, FOURTH
EPISODE Charlbury, Watney Collection (*attr.*)

Plate 145. PORTRAIT OF A YOUNG MAN Paris, Louvre (*attr.*)

Plate 146. DOOR OF THE SALA DEGLI ANGELI Urbino, Ducal Palace
(attr.)

Plate 147. *Detail of plate 146*

Plate 148. *Detail of plate 146*

Plate 149. CHARITY and HOPE Urbino, Ducal Palace (*attr.*)

Plate 150. FAITH and PORTRAIT OF FEDERICO DI MONTEFELTRO
Urbino, Ducal Palace (*attr.*)

DATE DUE
